A plastic timeline

1856

Alexander Parkes uses cellulose from plants to invent Parkesine.

1880

Plastic replaces animal horn and tortoiseshell as the most popular material for making combs.

1897

Casein plastic, made from milk, is invented in Germany.

1870

John Wesley Hyatt produces a plastic called celluloid.

1907

Bakelite is invented by Leo Baekeland. It is the first synthetic plastic.

1892

An artificial silk fibre called rayon is made from cellulose.

1956

The first cooking pans with a non-stick plastic coating are manufactured.

1935

A plastic fibre called nylon is invented by Wallace Carothers.

2011

The new Boeing 787 airliner has more plastic parts than any other airliner before.

1932

Perspex, also known as plexiglass, is invented. It is used as a replacement for glass.

2001

Helios, an experimental unmanned aeroplane, made mainly of plastic, reaches world record height of 29,524 metres (96,863 feet).

1940

A new synthetic rubber helps supply huge numbers of rubber tyres during World War II.

What is plastic?

UNIT

Hydrogen atom

Carbon atom

POLYMER

Plastic is a material such as nylon, PVC or polythene that can be moulded into a new shape while it is soft. It then sets, keeping its new shape. The word 'plastic' comes from a Greek word, *plastikos*, meaning 'able to be moulded or shaped'.

Everything you can see and touch is made of invisibly tiny particles called atoms. They're so small that you can't see them, no matter how good your eyesight is. Atoms often join together in small groups called molecules. Most molecules contain just a few atoms. Plastic is different. It's made of very long molecules. Each molecule looks like a length of bicycle chain. It has hundreds or thousands of identical units joined together to form a long chain called a polymer. These long chains can slide over each other, making the plastic soft and easily shaped when it is hot, and then they link together when it cools, locking in the new plastic shape.

Author:

Ian Graham took a degree in applied physics at City University, London. He then took a graduate diploma in journalism. Since becoming a freelance author and journalist, he has written more than 250 children's non-fiction books.

Artist:

David Antram was born in Brighton, England, in 1958. He studied at Eastbourne College of Art and then worked in advertising for 15 years before becoming a full-time artist. He has illustrated many children's non-fiction books.

Series creator:

David Salariya was born in Dundee, Scotland. He has illustrated a wide range of books and has created and designed many new series for publishers in the UK and overseas. David established The Salariya Book Company in 1989. He lives in Brighton with his wife, illustrator Shirley Willis, and their son Jonathan.

Editor: **Caroline Coleman**

Editorial Assistant: **Mark Williams**

Published in Great Britain in MMXVI by
Book House, an imprint of
The Salariya Book Company Ltd
25 Marlborough Place, Brighton BN1 1UB
www.salariya.com
www.book-house.co.uk
ISBN: 978-1-910184-94-3

S·A·L·A·R·I·Y·A

1 3 5 7 9 8 6 4 2

A CIP catalogue record for this book is available from the British Library.

Printed and bound in China.

Visit our website at **www.book-house.co.uk**
or go to **www.salariya.com** for **free** electronic versions of:
You Wouldn't Want to be an Egyptian Mummy!
You Wouldn't Want to be a Roman Gladiator!
You Wouldn't Want to be a Polar Explorer!
You Wouldn't Want to sail on a 19th-Century Whaling Ship!

PAPER FROM
SUSTAINABLE
FORESTS

You Wouldn't Want to Live Without™

Plastic!

Written by
Ian Graham

Illustrated by
David Antram

Series created by
David Salariya

BOOK HOUSE
a SALARIYA *imprint*

Contents

Introduction   5

A world without plastic?   6

Before plastic   8

The first plastics   10

Science to the rescue!   12

Plastics take off   14

Into the Space Age   16

It's a plastic world!   18

Plastic fantastic!   20

Make it from plastic   22

Super strength   24

Plastic problems   26

Looking into the future   28

Glossary   30

Index   32

Introduction

Look around your home or school and you'll see plastic everywhere. It's in your computer, mobile phone, television set, toys, games, pens, sports equipment and even the books you read. Your clothes, carpets, furniture and even the paint on your walls probably contain plastic too. Look in your kitchen. You'll find a lot of plastic there. Plastic plays such an important part in everyone's life today that it's difficult to imagine what the world would be like without it. Many of the things you do every day would be different, or more difficult or maybe even impossible if plastic had never been invented. And many of the things you buy would be much more expensive without it. You really wouldn't want to live without plastic.

A world without plastic?

Today, nearly everything is either made of plastic or has some plastic parts. There are lots of different types of plastic. Some are soft, others are hard. Some are see-through, others aren't. Some are smooth and glossy, others are dull and rough. And they can be made in white, black and every colour of the rainbow. The story was very different just over a hundred years ago. The many different types of plastic we have today hadn't been invented yet. Can you imagine what it would be like if plastic had never been invented? We might not have things like mobile phones, computers or the Internet.

HOPE YOU LIKE BAGGY CLOTHES! Without plastic, the synthetic fibres that give modern clothes their stretchiness would not exist.

BEFORE PLASTIC, glue was often made by boiling up animal hooves and hides. Most modern glues contain some form of plastic.

WITHOUT PLASTIC, you probably wouldn't have computers, mobile phones or games consoles, because so many of their parts are made of plastic.

PLASTIC FURNITURE can be made in almost any shape; some would be difficult to make as easily or cheaply from other materials. Some couldn't be made at all.

A home without plastic

How it works

Horse hooves were used to make glue because they contain keratin (so do your fingernails!). When hooves are melted in boiling water and acid is added, the keratin melts and forms thick, jelly-like glue.

Wool

Brass

Cotton

Cotton

Paper

Cotton

Glass

Leather

Wood

Wood

Wool

Wood

7

Before plastic

Plastic was not common in people's homes until the 1950s. Before then, nearly everything was made of traditional materials including wood, metal, stone, glass, leather and natural fibres. Small items like buttons and knife handles were made from ivory, horn and antler. These materials have been used for thousands of years. They have to be collected from wherever they can be found in nature and then processed to change them into useful things. The people who process them have years of experience in working with natural materials. They know about each material's strengths and weaknesses. However, plastic is about to change all of this.

Wood for building

Wool for making clothes

PIANO KEYS used to be made of ivory from elephant tusks. Playing a piano is known as 'tickling the ivories'. Ivory from one tusk could make 45 keyboards.

BEFORE COMBS were made of plastic, they were made of bone or antler. Their teeth were brittle and often snapped off. Plastic combs have flexible teeth that last longer.

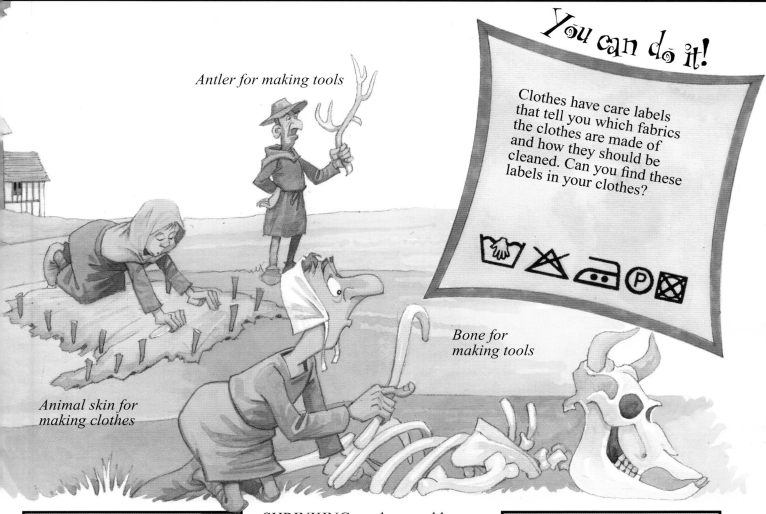

Antler for making tools

You can do it!

Clothes have care labels that tell you which fabrics the clothes are made of and how they should be cleaned. Can you find these labels in your clothes?

Bone for making tools

Animal skin for making clothes

SHRINKING can be a problem when washing clothes made of natural fibres, especially woollen items. Clothes with synthetic fibres endure repeated washing.

SITTING PRETTY.
Cushions, chairs and soft toys used to be stuffed with straw, wool, wood shavings, sawdust, feathers and horsehair. Today plastic fibres and foam are used.

The first plastics

The first plastics are made from natural materials. One of the strangest is shellac. It is made from a substance called lac, which is produced by an insect, the lac bug. About 100,000 lac bugs produce 500 grams (1 lb) of shellac. Shellac can be moulded to form all kinds of different shapes. The first records (music discs) in the early 1900s are made of shellac. Another early plastic is Parkesine, patented in 1856 by Alexander Parkes. Parkesine is made from cellulose, a substance that comes from plants. The first photographic film is made from long strips of a clear plastic called celluloid, invented in the 1870s. One plastic is even made from milk! If modern plastics had not been created, we might still be using plastics made from natural materials.

SHELLAC RECORDS are very popular, but very brittle. Many of them end up cracked and broken. Plastic 'vinyl' discs introduced in the 1930s are not as brittle, so last much longer. They quickly replace shellac discs.

THE LAC BUG produces a red liquid called lac, which sets on tree branches to form a glassy red material. It is collected, purified and processed to make shellac.

Thank you!

It's shellac, from creepy crawlies!

You can do it!

Ask an adult to heat a cup of milk.* Don't let it boil. Add two tablespoons of clear vinegar. Stir until lumps appear. When cool, squash them together. You've made milk plastic!

*SAFETY: take great care not to splash or spill hot milk!

THE FIRST PHOTOGRAPHS are made one by one, on metal plates or sheets of glass. Celluloid film makes it possible to take photographs quickly enough to produce the first movies.

BRITISH QUEEN MARY (1867–1953) owns plastic jewellery made from milk! Milk contains a substance called casein. This is processed to make the plastic, called casein plastic or Galalith.

11

Science to the rescue!

In the early 1900s, scientists start looking for new ways to make plastics. Instead of processing natural materials, they combine chemicals to make new ones. These plastics, created by scientists in laboratories, are called synthetic plastics. The first synthetic plastic in 1907 is named Bakelite after its inventor, Leo Baekeland. By the 1920s, radios, cameras, jewellery, light switches, electrical plugs and clocks are being made from Bakelite. In the 1930s, Wallace Carothers creates a famous plastic called nylon, which is still in use today.

SHIRTS MADE OF NYLON are popular, but not for long. Electric charges build up on the fibres and give you an electric shock when you touch something metal, like a door-handle. Ouch!

New uses for plastic

BAKELITE ARRIVES just as an invention called radio becomes popular. Millions of Bakelite radios are sold from 1920 to 1950, before television becomes widely available.

SO MANY THINGS are made of Bakelite that it becomes known as 'the material of a thousand uses'. You can even have a coffin made of Bakelite!

SOME PLASTICS created in the early 1900s are still used today. Look inside any small machine and you'll probably find gearwheels and other parts made of nylon.

WALLACE CAROTHERS (1896–1937) was an American chemist credited with the invention of nylon.

Wallace Carothers

Nylon fibres

Top tip

Nylon is used for making gearwheels because they're quieter than metal gearwheels, they don't need to be oiled, they don't rust and they last longer.

13

Plastics take off

During World War II (1939–1945) all sorts of materials are in short supply, including rubber. Scientists are given the job of creating a new material that can be used instead of natural rubber. They succeed in making a stretchy rubber-like plastic. They manufacture other new plastics too such as Kodel, Terylene and Dacron. After the war, millions of people are rebuilding their lives in new homes. Factories start making all the products they need, using the new plastics created in the 1930s and 1940s. It is around this time that plastic bottles begin to replace glass bottles. Plastics really take off.

THERE ISN'T ENOUGH natural rubber to make tyres and other rubber parts for all the trucks, planes and machines during World War II. Scientists create synthetic rubber to solve the problem.

IN THE 1930s, a new see-through plastic called Perspex is used to make cockpit canopies of fighter-planes. Bulletproof glass is also made by placing plastic between two sheets of glass.

14

DANGER! Before bottles were made of plastic, they were made of thick, heavy glass. These bottles shatter if dropped or knocked over. Plastic bottles are much safer – they bounce!

You can do it!

Are any parts of your toys not made of plastic? Why do you think they aren't plastic? They might have to be stronger, harder or springier than the plastic parts. Or is there another reason?

MORE DANGER! You wouldn't be so keen to play with toys if plastic had not been invented. Some toys are made of tinplate and lead. Tinplate has sharp edges and lead is poisonous.

Ouch!

15

Into the Space Age

Mass-produced plastic products reach shops in the 1950s just as the first spaceflights hit the headlines. Plastic is a Space Age material for a Space Age world. After the dark days of World War II, plastic makes everyone feel that the future has arrived. The first plastic products break more easily than sturdy wood and metal products and can't be repaired as easily, but it doesn't matter because new plastic products are cheaper to buy. It's the beginning of our throwaway lifestyle. Instead of repairing something, we throw it away and buy something new to replace it.

A PLASTIC HOOP called a Hula Hoop is a must-have toy in the late 1950s. The idea is to spin it around your waist and keep it going by swivelling your hips.

THE FIRST TRANSISTOR RADIOS, made of plastic, appear in 1950. Their sound quality isn't great, but they are very popular among young people, because they are so small and portable.

Mix one tablespoon of cornflour (cornstarch) with one tablespoon of water. Stir in a tablespoon of white craft glue (this contains plastic polymer). Let it stand and it turns into plastic slime.

BEFORE THE 1960s, dolls' heads were often made of china or porcelain. They broke very easily, so they had to be handled carefully. Plastic dolls are much tougher and so they last longer.

THE FIRST MODERN CREDIT CARDS are issued in the United States in the 1950s. These plastic cards make it easier for people to buy new products from shops.

17

It's a plastic world!

There are thousands of different plastics for making all sorts of products. Think of all the gadgets you enjoy using. Your game console, laptop, tablet computer and headphones all depend on plastic. Many of them have plastic cases, buttons and switches. The electronic circuits inside them depend on plastic too. The circuits are built on circuit boards made of plastic. Their microchips are sealed in plastic blocks. All sorts of electrical equipment, from table lamps to vacuum cleaners, work safely because of plastic. Their electrical wiring is covered with plastic to stop electric currents from escaping. Without plastic, life would be truly shocking. ZAP!!

STICK AT IT. Many of the glues used today, from craft glue to superglue, contain plastic polymers. As the glue sets, its long polymer chains lock together.

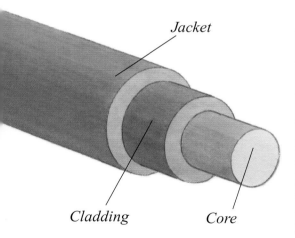

Jacket

Cladding   *Core*

LIGHT PIPES. The cables that carry telephone calls and computer information used to be made of metal. Now, many of them are made of thin strands of glass or plastic called optical fibres.

THE GLOSSY PAPER used for printing photographs and magazine covers is coated with plastic to make it super-smooth and shiny. The coating is also designed to help coloured ink stick to the paper.

PARACHUTES, yacht sails and hot-air balloons are made of a very strong plastic fabric called ripstop. Its fibres are woven together to make a fabric that will not rip or tear easily.

ULTRA-LIGHTWEIGHT PLASTIC has made it possible to build aircraft that were impossible to make in the past. Helios was an electric plane powered by the energy in sunlight.

Plastic circuit boards are covered with metal tracks. The tracks work like wires and connect the different parts of a circuit to each other.

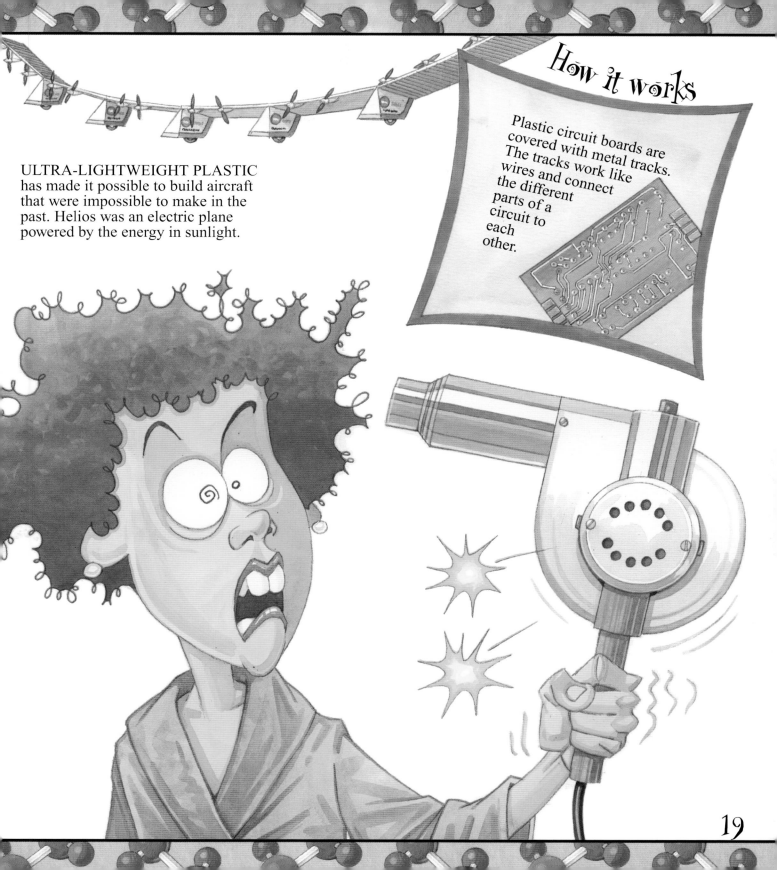

Plastic fantastic!

If it weren't for plastic, you'd have to work a lot harder at home. Smooth plastic surfaces are easy to clean with a wipe. Old wooden kitchen tables had to be scrubbed with smelly disinfectant to keep them clean. Modern nonstick saucepans are easier to clean than old iron or enamel pans. In the bathroom, toothbrushes with plastic bristles are easier to clean than old brushes made of animal hair. Modern paints and varnishes contain plastic, giving them a hard-wearing, long-lasting, easy-to-clean surface. Without plastic, you'd have to repaint surfaces more often and spend much more time cleaning them. Plastic makes life much easier.

HOW WOULD YOU LIKE to brush your teeth with animal hair? It sounds disgusting, but before brushes were made of plastic, toothbrush bristles were made of stiff hair from a horse or boar.

IRON AND STEEL turn to rust if they get wet. They have to be polished or painted to protect them. Plastic doesn't rust, so it doesn't have to be polished or painted.

How it works

Iron and steel turn to rust because of a chemical reaction between the metal, water and oxygen in the air. Plastic doesn't rust because it doesn't react chemically with water and oxygen.

Iron chain

Plastic chain

OUTDOORS in damp weather, wood can rot quickly unless protected with a coat of preservative, varnish or paint. Now, there are doors and window frames made of plastic.

A STICKY PROBLEM. If there were no plastic sticky tape, you'd have to make do with tape made of paper or fabric. Paper tears and fabric tape is thick and ugly.

21

Make it from plastic

About 250 million tonnes (246 million tons) of plastic is made every year. Newly made plastic looks like brightly coloured gravel. To make things, it is heated until it melts. Chemicals may be added to make it harder, softer or a different colour. Gas may be blown into it to make foam plastic. The hot plastic is forced into a mould. The mould is cooled to harden the plastic. One moulding machine can make hundreds or even thousands of identical plastic products a day. A variety of different manufacturing methods are used, including injection moulding, extrusion, drawing and blow-moulding.

DRAWING. Fibres are made by forcing hot plastic through tiny holes in a disc called a spinneret (right). Cold water hardens them.

Plastic granules go in

EXTRUSION. Melted plastic is forced through a die (metal block) with a large hole in it. Plastic rods, bars and pipes are made like this.

INJECTION MOULDING. Melted plastic is forced into a mould. Cold water cools the mould. It splits open and the perfectly formed plastic product falls out into a waiting bin.

The spinneret is named after the part of a spider that makes silk.

Spinneret

Nylon

Water

Rollers

You can see how extrusion works by squeezing icing out of an icing bag. Alternatively, spoon some yoghurt into a plastic bag and cut off one corner. Then squeeze... GENTLY!

Plastic building blocks come out

BLOW-MOULDING. A mould closes around a tube of hot, soft plastic (1) and air is blown inside (2). The air forces the plastic against the mould. Bottles are made in this way (3).

Mould   Molten plastic   Air   Moulded bottle

(1)   *(2)*   *(3)*

23

Carbon fibre

1. MATS of woven carbon fibre are laid in a mould and soaked in resin (liquid plastic).

2. THE MOULD is sealed inside a plastic bag and the air is sucked out to squash the layers together.

3. THE MOULD, in the plastic bag, is heated in an oven called an autoclave to harden the plastic.

4. WHEN THE AUTOCLAVE has cooled down, the finished carbon-fibre part can be taken out. The plastic resin has set, locking the carbon-fibre mats together.

Super strength

Some plastics are strong enough to stop a bullet. Some of them are fireproof too. These plastics are used to make super-strong clothing to protect motorcyclists, firefighters and motor-racing drivers.

Ordinary plastics can be made stronger by combining them with another material. The new material is called a composite. Plastic composites are stronger than each of the materials they contain. Carbon-fibre reinforced plastic, also known as carbon fibre, is a composite material ten times stronger than steel and four times lighter. Sports equipment such as tennis rackets, golf clubs and ice-hockey sticks are often made of carbon fibre. It's used to make racing cars too.

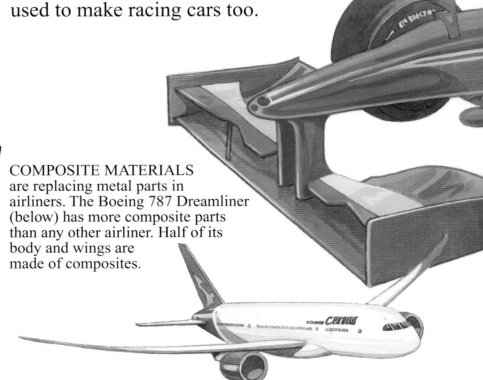

COMPOSITE MATERIALS are replacing metal parts in airliners. The Boeing 787 Dreamliner (below) has more composite parts than any other airliner. Half of its body and wings are made of composites.

Super-strong
fireproof suit

Carbon-fibre car body

SMOOTH PLASTIC boats slip through the water easily and quickly. The worms, barnacles and other sea life that often damage wooden boats can't get a grip on super-smooth plastic.

Plastic problems

Plastic has great advantages but it also has problems. In time, plastic parts and products break, wear out or just become unfashionable and they have to be replaced.

Old unwanted wood, food and natural fibres rot and iron rusts, but plastic can last for hundreds of years before it breaks down. One way to stop it piling up in waste dumps and polluting the land and water as it breaks down, is to use it again to make new things. This is called recycling. Another way is to burn it in a power station to make electricity.

OCEAN CURRENTS go round and round in circles in two parts of the Pacific Ocean, trapping rubbish in the middle (right). A lot of it is plastic.

Hmmm. That looks tasty!

ANIMALS might prefer a world without plastic. Countless turtles and seabirds have been killed by eating plastic in the sea, because they don't know it's bad for them.

LARGE plastic containers are re-used as water carriers in developing countries. The lightweight plastic enables people to carry water over long distances a little more easily.

Russia
Canada
Japan
Ocean current
USA
Pacific Ocean
Eastern garbage patch
Western garbage patch

You can do it!

Look for triangular recycling marks on plastic bottles in your home. Make a note of the different plastics you find. Which is the most common?

DID YOU KNOW that you might be wearing recycled plastic? Plastic drink bottles are recycled to make the fibres that fleece jackets are made of. It takes 25 plastic bottles to make one jacket.

PLASTIC BOTTLES can be recycled by using them to build houses. The bottles are filled with sand or mud. Empty bottles can also be used to build greenhouses for growing plants.

DIFFERENT PLASTICS are recycled in different ways, so recyclers need to know which plastics they have. To help, some products have a triangle mark with a number to show the type of plastic. It's called the Resin Identification Code.

Resin Identification Code

1	2	3	4	5	6	7
PETE	HDPE	V	LDPE	PP	PS	Other

Looking into the future

Scientists are still creating new plastics and improving old ones. Most plastics are made from chemicals that come from oil, but oil causes pollution and it will run out one day. Don't worry: you won't have to do without plastic. Future plastics will probably be made from natural materials, just as the first plastics were. They are called bioplastics. They're made from starch and cellulose produced by plants. Some bottles, packaging and car parts already contain bioplastics. There are also new plastics that heal when they are cut. Products made from them will never show scratches.

New technologies

CLEVER PACKAGING. There are new plastics that change colour when bacteria grow on them. Food packaging made of this plastic will tell you if the food inside is no longer safe to eat.

PRINT IT. Already people can make small plastic objects by using a 3D printer to print with. The printer makes things by building up one layer of plastic on top of another.

It's my new TV!

BENDY SCREENS. Nearly all screens on computers and other devices are made of hard, flat glass or plastic. Future plastic screens might be as thin and flexible as a sheet of paper.

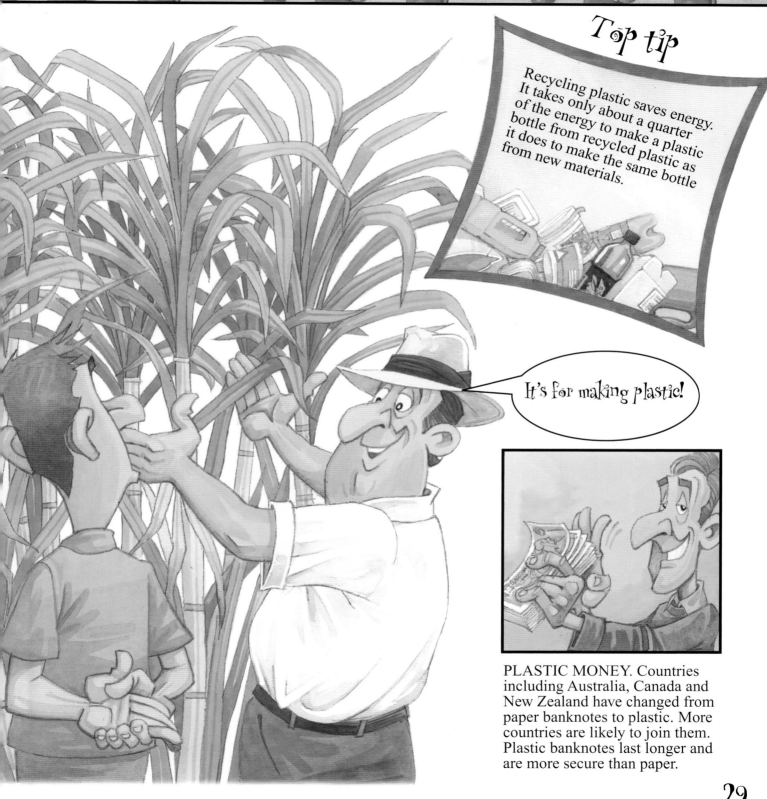

Recycling plastic saves energy. It takes only about a quarter of the energy to make a plastic bottle from recycled plastic as it does to make the same bottle from new materials.

It's for making plastic!

PLASTIC MONEY. Countries including Australia, Canada and New Zealand have changed from paper banknotes to plastic. More countries are likely to join them. Plastic banknotes last longer and are more secure than paper.

Glossary

3D Three-dimensional: having length, width and depth.

Atom The smallest particle of a chemical element.

Bacteria Microscopic living organisms. Many kinds of bacteria are harmless or useful to us, but some are dangerous because they cause diseases.

Blow-moulding A way of forming hollow plastic objects like bottles by closing a mould around a tube of hot, soft plastic and blowing air inside.

Canopy A covering such as the see-through top of a fighter-plane's cockpit.

Casein A substance found in milk.

Cellulose A substance found in plant fibres and the walls of plant cells.

Composite material A material made by combining two or more materials, such as carbon-fibre reinforced plastic, also known as carbon fibre.

Disinfectant A cleaning product, usually liquid, that kills bacteria.

Drawing A way of forming fibres by forcing plastic, or another substance, through tiny holes in a block of metal.

Electronic circuit A pathway along which an electric current can flow, usually through a series of electronic devices that use the electrical energy to do work.

Extrusion A way of forming plastic rods, bars and pipes by forcing hot, soft plastic through a block of metal with a large hole in it.

Factory A building or buildings where products are manufactured.

Fibre A thread of natural material (such as cotton), or synthetic material (such as nylon or rayon).

Gearwheel A toothed wheel. Also known as a gear or cog, usually found in small machines.

Injection moulding A way of forming plastic by forcing hot liquid plastic into a mould and then cooling it.

Lifestyle A way of living for one person or a group of people.

Manufacture To make products for sale, usually in large numbers.

Microchip A small package of electronic parts forming one or more electronic circuits in one small block of plastic. Also called a chip, integrated circuit, or IC.

Molecule A group of atoms linked together.

Monomer A molecule that is linked to lots of other identical molecules to form a long, chain-like molecule called a polymer.

Oxygen One of the gases in air. Oxygen makes up about 20 percent (a fifth) of the air you breathe. Most of the rest is another gas called nitrogen.

Pollution Unwanted and sometimes harmful substances in the environment, especially in the air or water.

Polymer A long, chain-like molecule made of lots of identical units called monomers linked together.

Space Age The period of history that began with the first spaceflight on October 4, 1957.

Starch A natural substance found in plants.

Superglue A very strong, quick-setting glue made of a plastic polymer called cyanoacrylate.

Synthetic Made artificially, by combining substances in a way that does not happen in nature.

Tinplate Thin sheets of iron or steel coated with a layer of tin.

Index

3D printer 28

A
antler 8
autoclave 24

B
Baekeland, Leo 12
Bakelite 12
banknotes 29
bioplastics 28
blow-moulding 22, 23
boats 25
Boeing 787 Dreamliner 24
bone 8
bulletproof glass 14

C
carbon fibre 24
Carothers, Wallace 12
casein plastic 11
celluloid 10, 11
clothes 6, 9
comb 8
composite 24
cotton 7
credit cards 17

D
drawing 22

E
electrical equipment 18, 19
extrusion 22, 23

F
fibres
  natural 8, 9
  synthetic 6, 9, 12, 23, 24, 25
film 10, 11
foam plastic 22

G
Galalith 11
glue 6, 7, 18

H
Helios plane 19
horn 8
Hula Hoop 16

I
injection moulding 22
iron 20, 21
ivory 8

L
lead 15

M
making plastic 22, 23
moulding 22, 24

N
non-stick saucepan 20
nylon 12, 13

O
optical fibres 18

P
parachute 18
Parkes, Alexander 10
Parkesine 10
Perspex 14
plastic bottles 14, 15, 23
plastic slime 17
plexiglass 14
pollution 26, 27

R
records (discs) 10
recycling 26, 27, 29
resin 24
resin identification codes 27
rubber 14
rust 20, 21

S
shellac 10, 11
spinneret 22, 23
steel 20, 21
sticky tape 21

T
tinplate 15
toothbrush 20
traditional materials 8

W
wood 7, 16, 21, 26
wool 7, 9
World War II 14

Top inventors of plastic

Alexander Parkes (1813–1890)
Parkes was born in Birmingham, England. He worked at a metal casting company, which made things by pouring molten metal into moulds. He dreamt up dozens of inventions, including new ways to process metal and strengthen it. Then in 1841 he invented a way of using rubber to make fabric waterproof. Fifteen years later, he invented the plastic that was named after him, Parkesine.

Leo Baekeland (1863–1944)
Leo Henricus Arthur Baekeland was born in Ghent, Belgium. He studied chemistry and became a chemistry professor. In 1891 he moved to the United States and two years later he invented a new type of photographic paper. In 1897 he became an American citizen. Then he experimented with chemicals to make new materials. In 1909, he announced his invention of Bakelite and set up a company to make Bakelite products. He retired in 1939 and died five years later at the age of 80.

Wallace Carothers (1896–1937)
Wallace Hume Carothers was born in Burlington, Iowa. He excelled in chemistry at university and went to work for the DuPont chemical company. There, he led a team of scientists who invented a synthetic rubber called Neoprene in 1930. Five years later he invented nylon.

Fire!

The first movies were photographed on film made from a plastic called celluloid. One of celluloid's disadvantages is that it catches fire very easily and burns fiercely. When it burns, it produces poisonous smoke. Even if celluloid doesn't catch fire, it breaks down chemically. The clear film turns yellow, becomes sticky and blisters. Eventually it falls apart altogether. The older it is, the more dangerous it becomes. It can even explode without warning! It's so dangerous that it can't even be thrown away. It has to be dealt with by experts. The oldest movies are kept in special fireproof storerooms until they can be copied onto modern film or recorded digitally. A safer plastic film replaced celluloid in the 1940s. It was known as safety film.

Although safety film doesn't burst into flames, it has another problem. After a few years, it begins to break down, giving off the tell-tale smell of vinegar. As the film breaks down, it shrinks and becomes brittle. Colours on the film begin to fade too. Films photographed on safety film can be rescued by copying them onto new film or recording them digitally.

Did you know?

- On July 14, 2007, a floating bridge 36 metres (118 feet) long was built from 14,100 empty 4-pint plastic milk bottles across the River Ouse in the city of Ely in England. It was the world's longest plastic-bottle bridge. The Mayor of Ely then tested the bridge by walking across it.

- Every year, between 500 billion and one trillion plastic bags are used worldwide. That's more than a million a minute! Some are recycled by weaving them together to make hats and shopping bags.

- Plastic takes so long to break down that nearly every piece of plastic ever made still exists today.

- DNA, the molecule inside our bodies' cells that carries the code that controls our growth and development, is a natural polymer.

The longest DNA polymers are huge. They can be hundreds of billions of units long.

- A 3D printer can build up a plastic model of almost any three-dimensional shape, even a model of yourself.